EASY BOGEY
HOW TO BREAK 90

THE AUTHORITATIVE GUIDE

SHOOTING IN THE 80S
WITH NO SWING CHANGES

BOB MADSEN, PGA PROFESSIONAL

ISBN: 978-0-9964031-1-5
First Printing: 2015

San Diego, CA USA

I would like to dedicate this book to some special folks:

My parents Ruth M. and Fred R. Madsen. Without them, I would never have even seen a golf course. My dad never saw me turn pro.

My Mom did. She saw me play and loved it. She also watched me teach a bit.

To my brother Russ who has always been there for me, supported me and loved me no matter what.

Bob Wallin, my father-in-law. Man, did he ever love his family and, secondarily, golf. Bob's my second favorite person ever to play with.

Barb Madsen, my wife and most favorite person to play golf with ever.

Walker Madsen. I love you Son.

Acknowledgements:

Thanks to all of the teachers, colleagues, and students who've helped in the evolution of this manual. I trust you know who you are and how much you've meant to this project. You've been the pioneers and coauthors.

In particular, I want to thank my friend and student Steve Montgomery (aka "Dr. Smooth"), who encouraged me to write this book, acted as my English instructor, edited every update, and assisted in making it as fun to read as possible. Steve has been by my side on this project since before it even had a name. He knows it upside down and backwards. Steve, I appreciate your commitment and enthusiasm almost as much as our friendship.

Special thanks also to my good buddy Rick Brand. Rick pushed me to stop talking about this project and actually start writing. Then he checked in with me almost daily, pushing me to keep going. On every revision he helped with the writing and proofreading. He and I also traveled together taking Easy Bogey on the road for test runs. He has been instrumental in proving it absolutely works.

Without Rick and Steve, this book would never have gotten done. Thank you both.

To those at Sycuan Golf Resort (formerly Singing Hills). Thank you for enabling me to practice my lifetime pursuits: playing and teaching. And now writing. I am indebted and will be forever grateful.

Finally, I owe a special thanks to Simon Meth who consented to practice Easy Bogey for an entire year in order to assist in the research. Extraordinary!

Contents

Let Me Introduce Myself

I started golfing early. I had a club in my hands as soon as I could walk. My parents and grandparents played golf. I started taking golf lessons in 1969 when I was nine years old and have been heavily involved in competitive golf ever since. I played junior golf in Southern California, high school golf at Westminster High in Orange County, and college golf at San Diego State University. I played in two U.S. Amateurs, a U.S. Publinks, four NCAAs, two PGA Professional National Championships, and four British Open Qualifiers.

I've won all of the various San Diego Chapter PGA Professional team and individual major championships.

I dreamed of playing on the PGA Tour, but didn't make it.

Thank goodness I fell in love with teaching.

I've been on the receiving end of a lot of instruction. Over the years I've taken probably 500 private lessons from seven distinctly different teachers. I still go see my favorite PGA Professional when I'm training. Taking lessons has taught me a lot about golf instruction.

I've been a full-time PGA Teaching Professional since 1991. I have given over 25,000 golf lessons, and have carefully observed amateurs in action for nearly thirty years including during five trips to Scotland.

Recognition has come along the way with the Horton Smith Award (for education) presented to me by the San Diego Chapter of the PGA of America. And I'm proud to have received the San Diego Chapter PGA Teacher of the Year Award three times.

I've also been teaching teachers through the years. I've presented at numerous PGA Section and Chapter Seminars, on topics such as:

- *Pace of Play*
- *How to Teach a Beginner*
- *The Full Swing*
- *Playing with Fewer Clubs*
- *Leave Their Golf Swing Alone!*
- *The Serious Business of Golf Breakthroughs*

I'm currently a Member of the hand-picked Southern California PGA Teaching Committee.

I've published dozens of articles that by all accounts have been enjoyed by the public and my peers. My readers and students have encouraged me to write this handbook.

Chapter 1

Tinkerville

I have been researching *Easy Bogey: How to Break 90* for a good twenty years. All the while, I've watched frustrated golfers spending too much time in a place I call Tinkerville.

Tinkerville means being lost with your golf game, always wondering what you're doing wrong. It's a place filled with endless swing thoughts and quick fixes, tips and pointers. It's where you read the golf magazines or watch the Golf Channel searching for answers.

Unfortunately, it's also where you rely on your buddies for advice, even though they're usually just as lost as you.

You've hit a "brick wall." You're stuck at a certain level of scoring, averaging above 90 shots a round. You love golf, but you've come to believe that you're never going to get any better. You tell yourself sometimes that you're comfortable where you're at.

You choose not to practice, saying "I don't want to practice bad habits." Yet you keep on looking and hoping to find something that will give you a breakthrough.

You're in Tinkerville, where it's "try this, try that"—and with little to show for your trouble.

Sound familiar? The trouble with golfing in Tinkerville is that, believe me, *you will not get better if you tinker.*

Yet there has been no real way out until now.

I know a way to help you break 90, not just once, but regularly. And I want to show you that in most cases it does not involve a difficult swing change.

I believe that, to shoot in the 80s, you need to go *back* in order to go *forward*—back to an old-fashioned sort of golf game, one that relies for scoring on smart course management and a sharp short game. In my view, these two golf fundamentals—course management and short game—are the way out of Tinkerville. The way to consistently lower scores. And the way to more fun with golf. Absolutely.

Chapter 2

Seven Reasons WHY You're Stuck

I have discovered the seven main reasons why average golfers are unable to break 90.

1. Over-aggressiveness.

As a full time teaching professional, I hear this all the time: "I paid my green fee. I'm going to GO FOR IT!"

Golf costs money. We all understand this. We want to get the most bang for our buck. Trouble is, the inherent danger in taking big risks is subtle. If you were snow skiing or rock climbing or surfing, the danger of injury or death might deter you from "going for it." Get in a little over your head and you might suffer grave consequences. Agreed? As a beginner, you would take it slow and easy.

Golf is different. You won't break your leg (or your neck) if you mess up a golf shot. Messing up in golf just gives you disappointment and frustration, along with zero progress. Still, most of you take unnecessary and counterproductive risks when you play, hoping for the joy of that occasional great shot.

• *Easy Bogey argues that the real joy doesn't come from the rare great shot, but from shooting consistently low scores you can be proud of.*

2. The golf you see on TV.

As you watch these follow-the-leader birdie fests on TV you come to believe this is "real" golf. You become inadvertently and sadly hoodwinked into thinking that golf is trying to par or birdie every hole. Although an amateur, you've been convinced you should try to play like the pros. This is like trying to perform 3rd degree Black Belt martial art moves even though you're not a master.

• *Easy Bogey asks you to learn to walk before you run.*

3. Too much golf instruction on TV, in golf magazines, and on the internet.

Commercially driven golf instruction offers endless tips, pointers, and quick fixes. You drink it up hoping something will "click" and improve your scoring.

Unfortunately, most of you don't have enough practice time to really ingrain anything on the driving range. Yet burdened by data about idealized moves with no time to train, you arrive at the course with a headful of really useless information and only stubborn old bad habits to rely on. Lack of practice time is real. Few of you really have time to groove a new golf swing.

• *Easy Bogey says you can learn to break 90 with the golf swing you have right now.*

4. An over emphasis on the full swing.

Golf's over fascination with full swinging is killing your chances of ever scoring lower. This term: "THE full swing" bugs me. When we say THE, it infers that there is some pie-in-the-sky singular ideal. This ideal is generated from watching the picture perfectness of the pros.

Now, pursuing a little bit of technical correctness totally makes sense to me. The problem is the over emphasis. The magazines are full of descriptions of the full swing, accompanied by frame-by-frame sequence photos. These pictures are pretty, but pretty useless to the 20 handicapper. Also, many teaching pros are very busy using video to analyze the full swing. The average golfer has no chance because he or she ends up overloaded with all these difficult-to-achieve angles, parts, pieces, and positions.

• *Easy Bogey says that the full swing is only a small part of what enables you to break 90.*

5. The unfortunate under emphasis on the short game in golf instruction today.

Back when I was a boy (my son Walker Madsen hates it when I use that phrase), there was no technological advancement in equipment whatsoever. So, there was no craving for new clubs. You weren't going to buy a better game by shopping for the latest driver or the hottest irons.

Nowadays, the major manufacturers have obviously made advancements. New equipment can help, no doubt.

But there's a balance between the latest equipment making a difference and a return to the tried and true way to lower your scores: skillful course management and short game.

• *Easy Bogey asks you to start chipping and putting your way to low scores. Competence from 40 yards and in is where better scoring happens. Not longer driving.*

True story: My dad, Fred Rees Madsen, was never in a hurry to use the driving range. He and I always went to the chipping green. We chipped and putted, always competing, for hours on end. We had chipping contests in the backyard. We invented chipping and putting games for in the house. I'm telling you, his short game was sharp! My Dad had the long game of a bogey golfer. He used hand me down clubs. He had the same beat up old leather golf bag and head covers for years. Nothing was pretty about his stuff or his long game. His scores, though, were very pretty. He shot in the 70s. He had so much fun beating his after-work golfing buddies with his short game that he never regretted the long game issues.

6. The total under emphasis of course management in golf instruction today.

Teachers, writers, TV show hosts, and other members of what I call the Golf Establishment, need to get away from swing tips and begin emphasizing playing lessons.

There are two types of golf lessons I want to highlight here: swing lessons and playing lessons. Golf swing lessons are held on the range. Playing lessons take place on the golf course and take way more than a half an hour. Playing lessons with the Pro often emphasize the secrets of course management: cleverly maneuvering the ball around the course. If the entire Golf Establishment would give more playing lessons, we'd watch everyone's scoring improve right away.

• *Easy Bogey asks for better thinking, resulting in smart strategic play.*

For example, during playing lessons I caddy for my clients. I advise on shot selection, club selection, thinking processes, etc. Pros know stuff about course management that amateurs don't. If you *think* more like a pro, you will score lower.

• ***Easy Bogey says that smart course management—responding to what the golf course is "saying"—is practically everything.***

7. Lastly, I need to mention what I call "dabbling."

Dabbling is another reason why golfers are not scoring to their potential. Dabbling means saying you're trying to get better without really doing something about it.

You're getting coaching from wrong sources like magazines and fellow competitors. This leads to Tinkerville. You're trying to "figure it out" without getting yourself a high caliber PGA or LPGA Professional and actually working at the game.

Keep in mind that you have chosen quite possibly the single hardest game on the planet. I recommend that you pursue the game most thoroughly. Learn the Rules better. Study golf course architecture. Research the history of the game. More complete understanding in anything is always rewarded. In golf, a greater breadth of knowledge will help you not just with your scores, but with your comfort level on the course and overall sense of belonging.

• ***Easy Bogey promises that dedication and knowledge will help you score lower.***

> *Golf is deceptively simple and endlessly complicated; it satisfies the soul and frustrates the intellect. It is at the same time rewarding and maddening — and it is without a doubt the greatest game mankind has ever invented.*
>
> — Arnold Palmer

These are the seven main reasons why breaking 90 has become so elusive for so many golfers. I'm sure you can think of some more on your own.

Chapter 3

What Does Easy Bogey Do, Exactly?

E asy Bogey is a proven approach that will immediately help everyone who is struggling to break 90. With a simple change in approach, you'll be consistently shooting in the 80s.

It is revolutionary for many reasons. Here are a few.

1. Easy Bogey means exactly what the name implies—it's asking you to *take it easy*.

Most of us were taught to "try-harder" when we're not doing well—you know, get an "E" for effort. But this approach doesn't work in golf. Why? Because trying hard to get the most out of every shot creates tension, and tension is what causes most flubbed shots.

You have to learn to treat the golf course more like an intriguing puzzle that you figure out patiently, humbly, and thoughtfully. Golf is not a strenuous wrestling match taken on physically.

• ***Playing Easy Bogey will help you relax and stop trying too hard.***

2. Easy Bogey will help you avoid double and triple bogeys. Blow-up holes are like a brick wall that keeps you scoring in the 90s or higher. You might be going along quite nicely in a round, and then you take a double or triple (or two or three) that balloons your score. Did you know that blow-up holes are as much a matter of poor judgment calls as they are poor shot making? When you set up to play a shot you know you have little chance of pulling off, you unconsciously tense up and apply extra effort. This pretty much kills your chance of success.

• *Playing Easy Bogey will help you relax, feel more in charge of your game, and minimize your blow-up holes.*

3. Easy Bogey will help you score lower in every game of golf you ever play. Course management is essential on every golf course on the planet. Bash away on the range if you must, but golf courses punish poorly thought out, wildly missed shots. Conversely, all golf courses reward thoughtful strategy. This is especially true on more difficult courses, and on courses you have never played before.

• *Easy Bogey has you taking fewer chances and playing smarter golf—and this means choosing shots you can actually pull off with no sweat.*

4. Easy Bogey will cut your practice time. You'll know to ask your PGA or LPGA Pro for more playing lessons and short game help. You can write the job description for your Pro. He or she should welcome your request for less swing analysis and less hard work on the range. Pros know that all bogey golfers really need is a little short game help and smarter thinking on the course. I'm just pointing out the obvious and being real honest about it.

• *Easy Bogey says that improving your decision-making does not require you to hit endless buckets of range balls. A shift in viewpoint is mainly what you need.*

5. Easy Bogey is the easiest and most natural way to improve your golf swing. Rhythm and balance are non-negotiable fundamentals in the golf swing, and they immediately improve when you can say to yourself, "This'll be easy. I can do this." Tension, effort, and strain are killers. The golf club will not tolerate "trying." You can't muscle up and push on it and get consistently excellent club and ball contact. Choosing to take on miracle shots only adds doubt and tension into your golf swing. Believe me, you'll hit better shots if you gamble heroically less often or maybe never.

• *Easy Bogey breeds consistent, carefree, and effortless golf swings.*

6. Easy Bogey teaches you the same course management principles elite players use. College All-Americans, amateur champions, and professional golfers are certainly not playing Easy Bogey. Yet all these top-level players use course management in every round they play. Granted, scratch players have a tremendous amount of hard-earned physical skill, but just as important is their wisdom and patience in their shot selection. They are (along with their caddy), thinking every shot out before they select a club. They're good at the game of golf as much because of their mind as their ball-striking. For example, a scratch player does not go for a hole location that's near water from 170 yards. There's too much risk if the errant shot ends up costing a penalty stroke. The play for an expert in this case is away from the hole into the fat part of the green (Circle B, as you will see later). Easy Bogey golfers do the same thing, only they play to the throat of the green (into what I call Circle C), in front of any lurking trouble.

• ***Easy Bogey absolutely insists that course management scoring secrets are available and essential to every golfer.***

7. Thus, Easy Bogey decision-making principles are what help even 10–15 handicappers eventually get down to single digit. Playing risky shots for the wrong reasons is what's keeping all golfers from scoring lower.

• ***Easy Bogey could easily be renamed: "How Everyone Can Take Six to Ten Strokes off Their Score."***

Chapter 4

Taking Charge

I f you are a bogey golfer trying to par every hole, you have a problem. It just doesn't make sense. Can you see the contradiction? Would a high jumper raise the bar to some impossible height and continuously fail? No. Easy Bogey asks you to lower the bar for a while and hop over it successfully a bunch of times.

You simply start by changing your golfing "bar height" to 90, and commit to eighteen well thought out bogeys.

In other words, switch your personal "par" to 90. That's right: the goal is to just make bogey on every hole without even trying—thus, *easy* bogey. Scoring eighteen bogeys will give you 90. This gives you eighteen strokes to play with, leaving you with eighteen easy, fretless scoring opportunities. Throw in a par or two and guess what?

To reinforce your goal of making easy bogeys, it can be helpful to customize your scorecard on practice rounds. Before you tee off, just cross out the normal par numbers on the Par line and pencil in the bogey number on the line above or below.

Let's say that, on your home course, hole number one is a 383 yard par four. On your card (when you're practicing Easy Bogey) it will be a 383-yard par *five*. That means you can take three shots to get on with no risk at all. (See page 49 for an illustration.)

Of course, for official rounds the scorecard approved by the course Committee should always be used.

You can plan for bogeys this way for the whole round, but you can also do this in your head for individual holes. Looking at a monster 460 yard par 4 into the wind? Rethink the hole and play it as your own personal par 5. Facing a 200 yard par 3 guarded by water or deep bunkers? Instead of lashing away with your driver or 3-wood, think of it as a short par 4. That's right, you might *lay up* on a par 3! Off the tee, hit a short iron to a safe spot in front of the green, then use your short game to get up and down for a bogey—and maybe a par once in a while. This way you avoid a double or triple…or worse.

There's a bigger lesson here: the course is not in charge of your decision-making. *You are.* I want you to be in charge of your game and in charge of how *you* play the course. In order to accomplish this, you're going to switch temporarily to an achievable target score. You don't have to make any pars to shoot 90!

• *Easy Bogey says you play the course; the course doesn't play you!*

SPECIAL NOTE: Change the par to 108 if you're more of a double bogey player. This is a great option for beginners, for shorter hitters, or for those with special challenges.

Chapter 5

The Secret to Scoring Low

T he secret to scoring low is to avoid scoring high.

The way to avoid high scores is smart course management. Double and triple bogeys—those blow-up holes that are killing your rounds—are not primarily the result of poor golf swings. They're more than anything the result of the risky shots you're choosing to play.

When I was playing college golf at San Diego State University, my coach was Dr. Frank Scott. "Scottie" was like a father to me and a wise man. One thing he tried to teach us was that double bogeys were unacceptable. He considered them to be inexcusable mental errors. At the end of a tournament day, once the van was loaded and shut, he would utter "Well?" That was the double bogey call. Each of the men on the team had to confess how many doubles he'd made. If I'd made a couple, I'd say, "two." Then I would hang my head and hope one of my teammates might have made three or more—thus hurting the team more than I had—and lessening my shame.

Obviously, I didn't always appreciate the value of course management. After seven years as a scratch golfer I finally realized that I was wrongly trying to score low on every hole. I didn't know any better. I was trying to make every shot perfect. With the help of coaches, and my observation of better players, I learned I was taking unnecessary risks. In professional golf this is not only stupid, it hurts the payday. Recreational golfers suffer otherwise. The scorecard doesn't lie.

Even single digit handicappers do not play heroically. They navigate their ball like a pool player, always skillfully setting up the ball for the next shot.

The most important shot in golf is the next one.
—Ben Hogan

I was slow in realizing the value of Mr. Hogan's words.

I've always taken a caddy with me whenever possible. The caddy is part companion, cheerleader, and bag carrier. Most importantly, the caddy is a shot selection assistant. I train my caddies to ask plainly, "What if something goes wrong?" The Easy Bogey golfer wishing to break 90 must become a more intelligent caddy for him/herself.

Before you aimlessly blast away with all your might, please ask yourself, "What if something goes wrong?" It's critical that you learn to avoid

18

decisions that lead to big numbers. You're not going to make enough birdies to make up for all those blow-up holes.

> *Golf is said to be a humbling game, but it is surprising how many people are either not aware of their weaknesses or else reckless of consequences.*
>
> — Bobby Jones

• *Playing Easy Bogey means you never stop asking yourself, "What will happen to my total 18 hole score if something goes wrong with this shot?"*

I understand "Going for it" can be exciting. But is excitement what you are really after? Excitement is almost always hazardous to your score. Easy Bogey asks you to forego exciting shots and use strategy to eliminate doubles and triples, and make no worse than bogey. Playing smart will enable you to produce an eighteen hole score that you'll be proud of instead of just one memorable heroic shot now and then.

> *This is a game of misses. The guy who misses the best is going to win.*
>
> — Ben Hogan

Smart course management means always considering the safest possible shot. You might not always choose it, but that's absolutely where you should start as you begin to practice Easy Bogey.

The golf course is always presenting opportunities for making a good decision. Here are a few examples:

- If there's a deep bunker lurking, play away from it.

- Is there out of bounds on the right? Play left.

- Faced with 220 yards over water? Lay up short or go around.

- Tee off with a five wood just to put the ball in play.

- Easy Bogey says you don't always have to hit a driver.

- Steer clear of hazards completely. Hazards involve penalty strokes. Penalty strokes are score killers.

- Chip it out sideways when you're in the trees. Rattling your ball around in the trees is asking for a lost ball and/or a double bogey.

- Don't go flag hunting from 100 yards; just put the ball on the green and take your two putts.

- Hit a 5-iron for your second shot on par 5s instead of bashing away with your 3-wood.

- Play from the forward tees for a few rounds. Make it easy on yourself to break 90.

I know what you're thinking: "That sounds boring."

Here's the deal. Once in a while you will actually "hit a good one." You may make that cool birdie from the back tees you can brag about. I get it.

Unfortunately, high scores happen when that risky shot doesn't come off. It's that simple: if you don't learn to play well thought-out shots, the course will punish you with high scores.

• ***Easy Bogey says that low scores require boring simple doable shots. Sorry.***

We're talking about the secrets of course management and lower scores. We're not talking about the secrets of exciting, miracle, shot-of-a-lifetime golf.

The golf course architect employs many features in course design, including trees, hazards, OB, mounding, slopes, ditches, rough, and all too often forced carries that unfortunately demand heroics. These features are often beautiful, but the truth is the architect also puts them there to bewilder and distract you. Look at them and admire their beauty; but the smart golfer learns to note these features, read them, and play accordingly.

> *The woods are full of long drivers*
> —Harvey Penick

The golf course architect is talking to you at all times. The architect is really saying two things. On the one hand, he's luring you with "Go for it! You could get a birdie." On the other hand he's silently telling you, "Lower your risk. Don't gamble. Play to the BIG WIDE trouble-free open areas and I'll give you a bogey."

• ***In Easy Bogey, you learn to listen to the second message.***

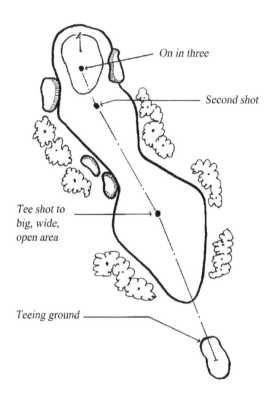

On in three

Second shot

Tee shot to
big, wide,
open area

Teeing ground

• *Easy Bogey insists that playing bravely involves risk. If you're too brave or unrealistically optimistic, your scores will suffer.*

Smart strategic play has a parallel in the field of wealth management. It's called "managing downside risk." It's a phrase I learned from a student of mine, who is also a trusted financial advisor. As I introduced him to Easy Bogey course management, he quickly saw how it related to his business.

He asked me, "What could happen if you take on too much risk with your family savings? You could lose it all!" His advice: **"You always need to manage your downside risk."**

I immediately loved the concept. That's it, exactly.

Chapter 6

Go for the Throat

S mart course management helps you stay out of trouble with your drives and fairway shots, but it's especially valuable with approach shots to the green. You have options, you know, when shooting for the green. Do not just go for the flag because you think, "Well, I ought to be able to." This is asking for trouble if you wish for a lower index. Learn to be totally honest with yourself about your skill level on approach shots.

• *Easy Bogey says that if you catch yourself thinking "I ought to be able to" you're about to play a shot that's beyond your capabilities.*

Easy Bogey asks you to stop going for the green. Instead, learn to read the golf course architect's mind. The architect is usually giving you a trouble free target area down in front of the green. This area is called the entrance or throat and it should almost always be your target.

Learn to listen: the architect is saying, "Just put it down in front here and I will give you your bogey."

• *In Easy Bogey you go for the throat. Then you simply pitch on and two putt.*

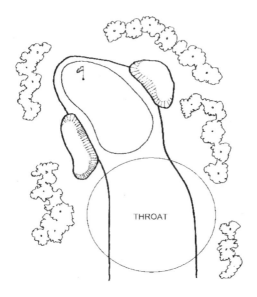

You'll even make a few one-putt pars and start to break 90—if you've put in some short game practice.

Start noticing this risk-free portion of fairway in front of most greens. Playing to this entranceway keeps you short of all the troubles usually clustered near the green: bunkers, deep rough, fall-offs, and water hazards. Playing safely into the throat of the green thus simplifies your short game shots. With Easy Bogey you can say goodbye to those nasty greenside shots that all too often turn what could be a sure bogey (or better) into a blow-up hole. Difficult shots such as...

• Flop shots over bunkers and mounds, those touchy and treacherous high soft pitches often played these days with a 60-degree lob wedge. They're what we used to call "cut shots" where you had to fancifully cut the legs out from under the ball with flippy wrists. The 60-degree wedge was invented to help with this.

• Buried lies in bunkers that result from highflying shots plugging deeply into greenside sand, and making for very difficult and specialized bunker shots.

• Explosion shots and mini-flops out of deep greenside rough, requiring exceptional touch and technique.

All these (and more) delicate and often costly short game challenges can be eliminated by playing your approach shots smartly down in front of the green.

• ***Easy Bogey says that if you can't break 90, you need to start laying up into the throat on just about every hole.***

Let me be clear: I don't mean playing to the *front edge* of the green. That's too close to danger and will often get you into trouble. I want you to play your approach shot down in front quite a bit *short* of the green.

To show you what I mean, let's do some quick math. If you have 170 yards to the middle of the green, you would subtract at least 25 yards. That'll get you into the area in front of the green and where, most often, you'll be left with an uncomplicated short game shot. Bogey (or better) will be yours.

Why 25 yards? Most greens measure somewhere around 30 yards in depth. So, it's usually 15 yards less to get to the front edge. Subtracting 25 yards keeps you *short* of the front edge. For example, if you have 170 to the middle, you only have 145 yards to the safe spot in front of the green. In Easy Bogey, you'll hit a 145 shot. That'll leave you a simple chip or pitch.

NOTE: on some holes there's going to be a lake or a gully or something protecting the front of the green. When that's the case the architect has taken away the lay up and is saying "Show me what you've got."

Let me introduce you to something really special. I use this all the time with my students. I call it Circles A, B and C.

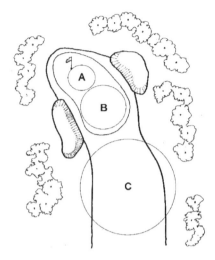

Circle A is an area right around the flagstick that a scratch player may occasionally take dead aim at.

Circle B is a larger and safer area, often what we call the *fat* part of the green. Circle B is where better than average players consistently play to. I am talking about low 80s and high 70s shooters.

Circle C is the BIG WIDE open area often well short of the green. It's another name for the entrance or throat of the green. Shooting for Circle C very often takes all the greenside trouble out of play.

• *Easy Bogey asks you to identify Circle C on every hole.*

Then you swallow your pride and play into Circle C. After that you pitch on and two putt. This smart strategic play is the essence of Easy Bogey.

After we get you breaking 90 every round, you'll have earned the right to give yourself permission to play for Circles A and B occasionally. But that's down the road. Okay?

For now, go for the throat.

Chapter 7

Short Game Proficiency

As you're hopefully starting to see, course management and short game are the two main ingredients to lower scoring. We've been discussing course management. Now let's look at sharpening up your short game.

You're in luck. Becoming proficient around the greens requires a lot less practice time than full swing changes do. It's proven. You can turn chipping, pitching, lag and short putting into offensive weapons with a minimal amount of time and effort. Something like 20 hours over a period of weeks. You're also in luck because most facilities have short game practice areas you can use for free.

Ask your local experienced and expert PGA or LPGA Professional for a short game lesson.

Founded in 1916, The Professional Golfers Association of America is the largest working sports organization in the world, comprised of more than 27,000 dedicated men and women promoting the game of golf to everyone, everywhere. The PGA serves your local "club pros" and is distinctly different and separate from the players on the PGA Tour.

Remember: personalized expert coaching ensures productive practice time.

Don't be too proud to take a lesson. I'm not.
— Jack Nicklaus

Now, I'm going to share some golf vocabulary that'll help you understand short game even a bit better.

Short game means shots from 40 yards and in: pitching and chipping, bunker play, lag putting, and consistently holing short putts.

A *pitch* is a short game shot most often played with a wedge, where some height and a soft landing are needed. Pitches are played when there is not much green to work with.

A *chip*, on the other hand, is a shot where the ball is bumped with a lower lofted club (often a 7 iron or even a hybrid club) using a very small swing. The ball comes off low, flies only a little ways and runs a lot. This bump and run shot is used when there is no reason to put the ball up high in the air.

Rule of Thumb: If it occurs to you to putt it, always putt it even if you're off the green. Using the putter practically eliminates the fat or skulled short game shot. You're left with only having to judge the distance. Big advantage!

Don't just pull out a wedge and think high shot when you are up around the green. Easy Bogey asks you to first think *low*, and play a high shot only if you have to. The putt from off the green is a secret weapon essential to breaking 90.

• *Easy Bogey rule: when near the green, putt whenever possible.*

Lag putting is critical to any player's success. This means a well-judged putt from longish range that leaves you only a mere tap in or little two or three-foot putt to sink. Good lag putters seldom leave themselves with a lengthy second putt. This is because they judge the distance and speed correctly, trickling the lag putt to a stop right next to the hole.

• *Easy Bogey advice: worry less about the read of the break and more on judging the distance.*

One other concept—*trapping* the ball—is vital if you want to become expert in the short game and an advanced Easy Bogey golfer. Now, most iron shots need to be trapped, but it's especially important in your short game. "Trapping" means the action of the club pinching or squeezing the ball against the ground, causing it to jump into the air with backspin.

Here's one way to explain what I mean. Picture a ping pong ball sitting still on a ping pong table. Now imagine doing a sharp karate chop down onto the back of the ball. Here's what happens. The ping pong ball jumps UP off the table (it doesn't have anywhere else to go) and it has backspin on it. Do you agree?

This jump with backspin happens because the ping pong ball is completely "trapped" against the table. The same thing has to happen in golf. One of the first things I might teach a student is the skill of correctly interacting with the ground. The descending club, the ball, and the ground are all together for an instant as in the karate chop. This is the only way to get the kind of pop you want off the club and the flight you need.

Truth is, practically every shot in golf needs to be trapped. This is not limited to the short game. But by practicing trapping the ball with your short game shots you'll get the feel of it more easily and you'll be able to transfer that feel to your longer shots.

There's definitely no lifting. There's no scooping. There's no need to get under the ball. With a little practice, you can learn to trap both your pitch and the chip shots, enabling plenty of lift and skillful play from all sorts of different lies.

Chapter 8

Madsen's Easy Bogey Discoveries

H ere's a summary of Easy Bogey principles. These are useful discoveries my team and I have made while exploring this new way to approach golf.

• "If it's exciting, it's probably WRONG!" Sounds defeatist. Sorry about that.

• Commit yourself to smart golf, not heroism.

• Fret is an indicator that strain is about to bleed into your muscles and interfere with your rhythm and balance.

• The shot you *want* to play is almost never the shot you *should* play.

• Is the play you're about to make filled with any fear, doubt, or worry? If so, go to another play.

• Decide on the play that truly brings you the most comfort and relaxation.

• Always make humble course management decisions. They lead to more consistently effortless golf swings.

• Trying too hard is bad. It leads to forcefulness.

• Relaxed muscles allow the club and the arms to swing freely.

• Expert and humble course management decisions will be kinder on your body.

• Worry less about what others think.

• Often solitude is best when trying something new. Go out and play golf by yourself. Find out when the course is not crowded. Walk, enjoy yourself, and make me 18 bogeys.

• Find practice partners who "get it" and can provide support as you go about doing things a bit differently.

• Making Easy Bogeys usually depends on that first putt ending up close to the cup. Spend time emphasizing speed control on long putts. Pace is everything.

• Be willing to give up a stroke. Make a concerted effort to avoid throwing away two or three.

Remember: you don't have to make any pars to shoot 90!

Chapter 9

Absolute Killers

G olf requires and rewards excellent balance and fluidity. And this is where Easy Bogey principles will do your golf swing the most good.

1. Strain is an absolute killer. Good decisions remove strain. Playing to big wide open areas frees your muscles from strain. Freedom from strain allows you to have better balance and fluidity. The arms can swing freely when you're playing relaxed shots to comfortable areas instead of tensing up trying to thread the needle or play some heroic shot.

• *Easy Bogey suggests you relax. And when you think you're relaxed enough, relax some more.*

2. The urge to bash is another killer. We all want to blast it. The urge to hit hard might even be grooved into our caveman DNA. Easy Bogey course management lessons breed swings that are effortless, easy, and graceful. You do not need a long drive to make bogey easily. Nor, as you will read about later, do you need a long drive to shoot in the low 80s. I am on a mission to eliminate off-balance jerky golf motions filled with strain. You do not need to kill it. Trying to bash the ball is absolutely ruining your chances to score low. Men, check your alpha male attitude in the parking lot. Bashing is not golfing.

I get as much fun as the next man from whaling the ball as hard as I can and catching it squarely on the button. But from sad experience I learned not to try this in a round that meant anything.
— Bobby Jones

3. Another killer is what I call being "ball bound." This is when too much of our interest and attention is on the ball. Our eyes are on the ball. We feel like we have to do something *to the ball.* Brace yourself for what you are about to hear: *The ball is not the target.* We must commit to learning little by little to disregard the ball and simply swing through to a balanced finish. In other words, you need to swing as if *there is no ball.* In games like baseball and tennis I might say "keep your eye on the ball," as hand-eye coordination is a must. In golf, however, attention on the ball is a killer. It breeds an urge to hit (or lift or scoop or pound or kill).

I always like to see a person stand up to a golf ball as though he were perfectly at home in its presence.

— Bobby Jones

The Easy Bogey course management approach is a platform you can use to explore the freedom and consistent ball striking that's available when you focus on the target and allow the ball to get in the way of the club head. More like a free throw shooter in basketball or a field goal kicker in football. Can you imagine? For the free throw shooter, the ball is not the target. Imagine looking at the ball while shooting a basketball. Attention is on the hoop, not the ball. For the field goal kicker, the ball is not the target. The goal posts are the target.

4. And a last killer is thinking you need to HIT the ball. Maybe the single most valuable piece of ball striking advice I can give you is *swing, don't hit.*

> *Hit it with your practice swing.*
> — Sam Snead

I'll explain what I think Mr. Snead might have been getting at. You know that feeling of just practice swinging through air? It's easy right? Your body is on balance and moving with complete fluidity. *No effort.* That's what he is talking about. Tough to do when the ball is there, for sure, but if you're truly more interested in your target—where you're shooting for—instead of just attacking the ball, you'll be more able to hit it with your practice swing.

If the ball is not the target, then what is? On par 4s, the target is the big and safe, smart area of the fairway off the tee. On par 5 second shots, it's the big wide lay-up area maybe 100 yards short of the green. Next, on all holes, it's the entrance or throat down in front of the green. Then the green itself once you're close enough to play onto it. And finally it's the area around the hole, if you're putting from long range—or the hole itself if you're putting from short range.

Those are some of the absolute killers. Now on to some other challenges we all face.

Chapter 10

"But Bob..."

T his chapter deals with certain difficulties, complaints, gripes, grouses, and disagreements my students have expressed while playing Easy Bogey.

The commitment to being honest about your capabilities and using humble course management looks, on paper, like a piece of cake. In reality, it takes serious courage and perseverance. Here are a few of the issues that come up and some helpful hints on how to deal with them.

"But Bob, I'm not going to play scaredy-cat golf. What will my buddies think?" Being worried about what others think is not really healthy at any time. In the case of Easy Bogey it is essential to let that go. Are you trying to score lower and have more fun? Or are you truly more concerned with the opinions of others?

"But Bob, if I play for bogey, how am I ever gonna score LOW? Today could be the round of my life." Giving up what I call "This Could Be the Day" thinking is essential for Easy Bogey. Has trying for the shot or round of your life all the time worked out often enough to really make it worthwhile? Easy

Bogey golf leads to what most of us are really after: consistently better scores. Actually, many of my students have shot the round of their life after really adopting Easy Bogey.

"But Bob, that's not very exciting." This common complaint comes out of learners' mouths, or at least pops into their heads, when I'm caddying for them in playing lessons. I might say "Let's just chip it out from under the trees here and get out of trouble." The griping starts almost immediately. So I tell them "I'm sorry. If it's exciting, it is probably wrong."

"But Bob, that doesn't sound like much fun" is another familiar phrase preventing the correct intelligent play and consistently lower scores. What kind of fun are you really after?

• *Easy Bogey players find that shooting lower scores is what's really fun.*

> *If you try to fight the course, it will beat you.*
> — Lou Graham, 1975 US Open Champion

"But Bob, it's not my course management that's messing me up. I chunk [taking too much turf] wedges around the green all the time." Yep, I understand. You probably do chunk wedges all the time, but what really happened was you left yourself with an impossible shot that only Phil Mickelson could get up and down. High soft pitches from beside or beyond the green are not easy, even for single digit handicappers. They're beyond your skill level.

• *Easy Bogey asks you to miss the green down in front by design. Practice this a while, and those difficult short game challenges will simply disappear.*

Meanwhile, some professional lessons and productive practice on the high soft pitches might just be in order, since we all do end up in tough greenside situations now and then.

"But Bob, it's not my course management that's messing me up. I duff my second shots all the time." This one is a little more complicated. Very often the duffed or extremely wayward fairway shot is caused by having no good plan as to a target: that is, a place where you're going to play your next shot from. You're just whaling away trying to hit the ball far. This is not good. You may just be trying too hard (we all are) or you may not have enough of a lofted club for the lie you have. In addition, you may need a few range lessons and the accompanying practice dedication to attain more consistent and reliable ball-striking. For now, I'm asking you to make a second shot that's perfectly doable for you. For example, play a 6-iron down there into Circle C instead of trying to knock down the flag with your 5-wood from 200 yards.

• *Easy Bogey absolutely guarantees that your duffed shots will be fewer and farther between.*

"But Bob, I have a scramble tournament I have to play in." For this I usually tell the Easy Bogey student, "Please do not." Scrambles invite go-for-broke efforts and lots of bashing. Go-for-broke efforts and bashing are exactly the opposite of the approach I'm offering. If you must support a charity or participate in a work-related scramble, I understand. Just get back on the Easy Bogey project ASAP.

"But Bob, I want to go for the par." There are times when you can certainly do so. Judge wisely and consider VERY CAREFULLY the possible scoring disaster you might be asking for. Going for par (or for birdie) is a privilege you earn.

• *Easy Bogey requests: "for now, just make me 18 bogeys please."*

"But Bob, How am I going to get any birdies?" Short answer: you are not going to make any birdies. Well, that's not entirely true. Short game practice and expertise will reward you with an occasional chip-in from down in front of the green. You're not going to be making birdies because you're not going to be shooting for flagsticks like a scratch player. Instead, Easy Bogey asks you to play down in front of the green, taking the trouble out of play. You then send the ball up onto the green and two putt for bogey.

• *With Easy Bogey, we're talking about taking as many as 10 strokes off your average score by* **not** *going for birdies.*

Chapter 11

Maybe Even the Low 80s?

Madsen's Low 80s Formula: 6500 divided by 140.

I'll prove to you that if you can reliably move the ball 140 yards at a crack, you can shoot in the low 80s.

Don't believe me? Take the total yardage of your course, divide it by 140, and you will get how many shots it will take for you to cover that amount of ground. Then simply add 36 for the number of putts you'll need.

For example: 6500 total yards divided up into 140 yard chunks requires 46 shots. 46 shots + 36 putts = 82.

Do you have a club you can reliably move the ball 140 yards with? Give it a try. Go play with only that club, a wedge, and a putter. Then email me and let me know what happened.

Bob Madsen, PGA
Director of Instruction
Sycuan Golf Resort   El Cajon, California
bmadsen@sycuanresort.com

Here are a couple of true stories, told by two of my students/friends, about the amazing scores that are possible when you commit to playing Easy Bogey.

One Saturday afternoon a group of us had a playing lesson. Lots of hybrids off tees, lots of playing second shots for position, lots of hitting into the entrance of greens. That day I strung a lot of pars together and threw in a couple of birdies on par threes when I hit it close by mistake. Do I always play like that? Certainly not! But I now know what's possible…!

— Simon Meth

The two highlights of my golfing life I owe to Bob and Easy Bogey. In 2012 I won my flight (10-20 hdcp) of my club's senior championship. I won because playing Easy Bogey kept me out of trouble and I took very few penalty strokes. And then in 2014 I shot a 71—my all-time low—in a mini-tournament on a tough local course I rarely play. Again, I kept my ball in play and my short game was spot on. I drove home on cloud nine!

— Steve Montgomery

Golf is not only about scoring low and winning tournaments. Enjoying friends, having fun, and feeling good: these are the most important things Easy Bogey can give us, as a dear old friend of mine sums up beautifully:

> I was obsessed with golf for nearly thirty years, but I wasn't really enjoying myself. I was missing important stuff including: playing with fewer clubs, course design and course management.
>
> Since taking my first lesson from Bob in 1988, I've been obsessed with ENJOYING golf and the quest for genuine, valuable knowledge. His teachings and friendship have made me a better golfer and a better man. Even though he is eleven years younger than I, Bob Madsen is second only to my father insofar as his influence on my life. He is the best of men; patient, kind, thoughtful, and dedicated. A blessing to the game of golf.
>
> — Bruce Wilson, Rochester, PA

Thanks for spending this time with me, and best wishes.

Hole	1	2	3	4	5	6	7	8	9	Out
Yards	383	162	498	347	379	135	357	510	375	3146
	5	4	6	5	5	4	5	6	5	45
Par	4	3	5	4	4	3	4	5	4	36

	10	11	12	13	14	15	16	17	18	In	Total
	355	503	345	179	377	512	334	136	378	3119	6265
	5	6	5	4	5	6	5	4	5	45	90
	4	5	4	3	4	5	4	3	4	36	72

49

Made in the USA
San Bernardino, CA
14 January 2016